AF335467

TEAMWORK

ILFORD
SPALDING
Top-Flite 100
NM

Cooper Elementary Library

TEAMWORK

BY LOWELL A. DICKMEYER
AND MARTHA HUMPHREYS

An Easy-Read Sports Book

A GROLIER COMPANY

FRANKLIN WATTS 1984
New York | London | Toronto | Sydney

Photographs courtesy of Gary Gunderson (The
Litchfield Times): frontispiece, pp. 6, 9, 14, 16, 21, 22,
28, 37, 38, 42, 45, 46, 47; Ginger Giles: pp. 8, 11, 13,
15, 17, 18, 19, 25, 26, 30, 33 (top left), 44; Meryl
Joseph, Photographer: p. 33 (right); n.c.: pp. 33 (bottom
left), 34; UPI: p. 41.

Library of Congress Cataloging in Publication Data

Dickmeyer, Lowell A.
    Teamwork.

    (An Easy-read sports book)
    Includes index.
    Summary: Briefly discusses teamwork and how to be a
good teammate. Includes specific instructions for
basketball, football, baseball, tennis, golf, bowling,
soccer, and hockey.
    1. Teamwork (Sports)—Juvenile literature.
2. Cooperativeness—Juvenile literature. [1. Teamwork
(Sports)] I. Humphreys, Martha. II. Title.
III. Series.
GV706.8.D52   1984   796   83-21718
ISBN 0-531-04713-X

R.L. 3.5 Spache Revised Formula

Copyright © 1984 by Lowell A. Dickmeyer
and Martha Humphreys
All rights reserved
Printed in the United States of America
6   5   4   3   2   1

CONTENTS

GO, TEAM, GO!

A ball is hit sharply to the left side of the infield. The shortstop quickly scoops it up and shuffles it off to the second baseman. The second baseman fires to first for the second out. A double play! The crowd cheers!

This is teamwork. Teamwork is about good plays. It is also about players on the same team who do their best as individuals. Teamwork is about people who cooperate, hustle, and care about each other so that all of them are successful.

Teams are not just on playing fields. We find them everywhere. Families, clubs, schools, neighborhoods, and countries can all be teams. Whenever there are people working together, you will find a team.

Watch a school band. Each musician plays a special instrument. Each instrument blends with the others. Everyone performs together to create music for all to enjoy.

All sports involve teamwork. In individual sports like golf, singles tennis, boxing, or bowling it seems that one person makes all the decisions. He or she is responsible for the outcome. But if you look behind the scenes, you will find that there is a team working.

Coaches, trainers, friends, and families pass on their experience and support. These help the player. This is a kind of teamwork.

In team sports, the teamwork is more obvious. Coaches, trainers, family, and friends are on the team. They are behind the scenes. The only ones you see are the players working together.

Each player has his or her own job to do to help the team. Together, the defense and offense balance each other to form a working whole.

Being part of a team feels good. Practice is a necessary part of every good sports effort. Practice is better when it is shared. It is also more enjoyable to practice together. Some players have more abilities than others. They can help those who must work harder in the practice sessions.

When the team loses, everyone shares in the pain. But when the team wins, everyone celebrates.

HOW TO BE A GOOD TEAMMATE

Not everyone is a quarterback, a pitcher, or a centerforward. A team is not made up of eleven quarterbacks, nine pitchers, or eleven centers. To be a good teammate you must play where you play best, even if it is not where you want to play.

Those who score often receive all the glory, the headlines, and the applause. If you have skills, work hard, and score a lot you will be in the limelight. If you are also a good teammate, you will remember to include your teammates when you receive praise. They make it possible for you to perform as well as you do.

For those whose special skills are supporting the scorers, sometimes the only hand you will shake will be your own. But you know you are a good team member and that you have done your job well. And that makes you feel good.

Being a good teammate means helping each
other off the field as well. If friends have trouble with
homework, your special skills can help them.

Cooper Elementary Library

Teammates are always there to help, to encourage, and to assist each other whenever possible.

Being a good teammate means following directions, attending practices, and trying your best. You may not always agree with what your coach tells you to do. You may not feel like going to practice or taking care of yourself the night before a game. But your team depends on you to be at your best.

Being a good team member means supporting the team through losses as well as wins. No loss is the fault of any one player, no matter how poorly he or she played that day. No win is the result of one last-minute free throw. The wins and losses are the result of the play of the entire game. They are also the result of all that went before the starting whistle: the practices, the support, and the general feeling of the team. Team wins are not overnight successes. They are the result of hard work by everyone.

Healthy, well-rested, well-trained teammates perform better on the field. Members of a team who feel a sense of belonging to the team and enjoy the experience generally feel good about themselves and what they are doing.

BASKETBALL

Everyone loves to shoot the ball and make the basket. Sometimes it is better to pass the ball to a teammate. A team usually has more fun if all the members have a chance to score. One superstar cannot carry an entire team. Individual points are not as important as the final score.

Don't dribble the ball if a pass is better. Try not to hog the ball. Take your shot if you have one. If you miss the shot, there will be others. If you are in the best position to shoot, you owe it to your team to try.

If another player has a better shot, pass the ball to her. Then screen that player so she can have as much time as possible to improve her chances to score.

When the other team gets possession of the ball, get back on defense fast. Good team players hustle as much on defense as they do on offense.

Each player owes it to the team to improve her individual skills. She should work on her special talents and encourage others to improve their skills. Those skills which need the most work will require the most time. A good team player will take as much time as necessary to improve the level of her play.

In basketball, unlike most other team sports, the successful scoring of foul shots can make the difference between a win or a loss. Players should practice foul shots until they sink more than they miss. Players can do this at home, in the park, or at school as well as on the practice court.

FOOTBALL

Teamwork is obvious in football as soon as the ball is snapped. The players all seem to scatter to imaginary places on the field. A player who refuses to work hard or wants all the glory makes it very hard on the rest of the team. His lack of teamwork shows.

Every move in football is planned. Each player has a place to be and a time to be there. If one player does not do his job, the play may not work and the team falls apart.

Conditioning plays an important part in football. The player should train to be the strongest and fastest member of the team. Running, stretching, jumping, and muscle toning exercises all help the player to stay fit and perform well. A player who tries to shortcut conditioning usually tires too quickly. Or he will end up injured. A player cannot do much for his team when his leg is in a bandage.

Players on the sidelines can help the team, too. They can give encouragement to the players on the field. They must be mentally and physically ready to go in whenever they are needed. When the defensive unit is on the field, quarterbacks need someone to catch their warm-up passes. Guards and tackles may need to use someone's shoulder to practice the blocking motion. A place kicker needs someone to hold the ball for practice kicks. Place kickers are often kidded about their clean uniforms. They are in the game only for seconds, but those seconds can make the difference between a win and a loss.

BASEBALL

Baseball differs from other team sports because there is more emphasis on individual players. In other team sports, the action happens so quickly that a player can make a mistake and it is over and forgotten quickly. This is not true in baseball, where all eyes are on the player who may or may not make the catch, hit the homer, or steal the base. If he does, he's a hero. If he doesn't he's a loser.

For that reason, teammates must support each other. One day the pitcher may throw a no-hitter, giving the fielders little or nothing to do. The next day, the same pitcher may walk in the go-ahead run. The team would not last very long if his teammates blamed him for the loss.

The same fielder who makes an error at second base may also hit in the winning run in the bottom of the ninth. The batter who can barely break .200 may be the best first baseman in the league. Baseball depends on the special talents of individuals in order to put together a good team.

To play as part of the team, you train at your specialty. You watch for the signals, and you obey them. A good team member never tries to stretch a single into a double when the base coach tells him to hold up.

When you are at bat, if you are told to bunt, to sacrifice fly, or to take a pitch, a good team member will contribute to the team's effort instead of swinging for the bleachers and a possible home run.

In baseball, talking it up is very important. In the dugout and on the field it is good to say encouraging things to fellow players. The pitcher needs to know the whole team is behind him no matter how well he is throwing.

TENNIS/GOLF/BOWLING

Most of us think of tennis, golf, and bowling as sports for the individual player. Most of the players think of themselves as one person playing against one other person. They want to see which one of them plays the game the best.

All athletes need training. They get this from their coaches and trainers. They perfect their individual skills, learn new ones, and benefit from their coaches and trainers. No one knows all there is to know about a game. Even in individual sports, most successful athletes admit that they depend on the other people on their teams, for example, their coaches and trainers.

Tennis has its doubles, golf its tournaments, and bowling its teams. If players are good team members, they must practice skills, take care of themselves, and play their best game possible in order to help their team. They will not blame other members if they are having a bad day. Nor will they hesitate to ask for help for themselves if they need it. One of the benefits of team play in individual sports is the joy of winning when there are others there to share it with. People who share can also lessen the pain of defeat.

SOCCER

Soccer is an international team sport. It is the game that best shows the differences in team play within a single sport. Each country has its own style of play.

Brazil has a slow, deliberate game with sharp, crisp passing. Germany and Holland play a fast-paced game where ball-handling skills shine. Scotland's game is more physical and rough-and-tumble. No matter what the style is, all the teams are highly respected as groups whose teamwork flows.

For these teams it all starts at practice. Good soccer players bring their skills to practice. They work together in small groups to perfect their passing, heading, and juggling techniques. They are constantly talking, teasing, and encouraging each other.

Everyone goes through all the drills. There are mini-games between various groupings where the players work on strategy as well as fundamentals.

Learning to stay out of a play is as much a part of teamwork as knowing when to jump in.

Soccer does not have as much scoring as other team sports. Passing and patience make up most of the game. Each player must wait for the right opening and then react quickly to pass or to score. Every player has an area to cover, and the rest of the team is there to back him up if the opportunity strikes and the team can score!

HOCKEY

One of the most exciting moments in sports was the United States victory over the U.S.S.R. in the 1980 winter Olympics. All of us in the U.S. shared in that win, the gold medal, and the achievements of our underdog team defeating the Russians.

That team demonstrated teamwork at its finest. At no time did any team members want to quit. They worked hard and supported each other on and off the ice to come from behind and win that stunning upset.

YOUR TEAM

In math they tell you the whole is never greater than the sum of all its parts. In sports, that's not true. The whole is often greater than the sum of all its parts. Look at any championship team.

Certainly there are stars on any team. There are individual players whose skills seem to shine on the playing field. How many outstanding quarterbacks would there be without blockers, pass receivers, or play makers? How many good pitchers would there be without steady catchers and dependable fielders? There is never a score without an assist, never an assist without a block. And there would be none of these without good support from the coach and the bench.

Your teammates are also schoolmates, your family, members of your club, your neighbors, and your community. The things you learn that make your team winners will make the other groups in your life be more successful, too.

Just as you might not get to play the position you want on your team, you might have to give up other things you want for your school, neighborhood, and family. Not all the time, though. If you give up something you want sometimes, there will be other times when members of the group will give up something they want for you. It's called cooperation and compromise.

Add that to your best effort and practice in your skills, and you will be a valuable team member on every team you join throughout your life.

BELONGING TO A TEAM

Joining a team means bringing the best parts of you and sharing the best parts of your teammates for the benefit of the group.

Be a good team member in the classroom, on the playing field, in the neighborhood, and in the community. Be a winner.

INDEX

Cooper Elementary Library